GW01406585

Original title:

Creative Courage

Author: Annabel Swan
ISBN HARDBACK: 978-9916-87-744-9
ISBN PAPERBACK: 978-9916-87-745-6
ISBN EBOOK: 978-9916-87-746-3

Tidal Waves of New Perspectives

From depths unknown, the tides will turn,
New views arise, as lanterns burn.
Through salty spray, we learn to see,
The vast horizon setting free.

Each wave that crashes on the shore,
Whispers tales of what's in store.
With every crest, a chance to grow,
Embracing tides that ebb and flow.

A shift in sands, a fleeting glance,
Invites the bold to take a chance.
In rolling waves, we find our voice,
To ride the currents, forge our choice.

With open hearts, we dive right in,
Embracing what the tides begin.
For every wave that breaks with ease,
Brings forth a hum of mysteries.

So let us surf on visions new,
The world a canvas, vast in hue.
With tidal waves of fresh insight,
We'll paint the dawn, ignite the night.

Notes in a Minor Key of Bravery

In shadows cast by whispered fears,
We find the strength, confront the years.
Each note a testament, resound,
To all the hopes and dreams profound.

With courage sewn in every line,
We sing aloud, our spirits twine.
A melody of heart and soul,
Brings forth the light, makes us whole.

In minor keys, we learn to stand,
To face the world, to take command.
For bravery blooms in quiet space,
Each note a bridge, our saving grace.

Let echoes linger in the night,
As we embrace our inner light.
With every chord, let truth arise,
In harmony, we find our prize.

Though trials shape the songs we weave,
In minor keys, we still believe.
With bravery, our voices rise,
A symphony beneath the skies.

The Dance of Unconventional Paths

In steps uncharted, we convene,
A dance unfolds, wild and serene.
With twirls that break the rigid mold,
We move with grace, unique and bold.

The rhythm shifts, invites the brave,
To leap beyond what others crave.
In every turn, we find our way,
Through vibrant hues of night and day.

With every misstep, laughter flows,
In unconventional, beauty grows.
With hearts aligned, we twist and sway,
Creating art in our own way.

As shadows stretch, our spirits soar,
We dance on paths not walked before.
In every beat, our stories blend,
An endless journey without end.

So let us waltz in wild delight,
Embracing change, igniting light.
For in the dance of life, we find,
The strength to free our open minds.

Labyrinths of Aspiration

In mazes deep where dreams reside,
We walk the paths, our hopes our guide.
Each turn a choice, each bend a chance,
To seek the light, to find romance.

Through winding ways and narrow lanes,
Our spirits rise, absorbing gains.
In every corner, lessons learned,
As flickers of desire are burned.

With courage held, we forge ahead,
In labyrinths, our fears are shed.
For every stumble, every fall,
Reveals our heart, answering the call.

The journey's long, the goal unclear,
Yet passion whispers, softly near.
Through darkest nights and brightest days,
Aspiration paves the winding ways.

So let us wander, soul in hand,
Through secret paths, over shifting sand.
In labyrinths of dreams, we find,
The strength to reach beyond confined.

The Brush of Audacity

With colors bold, they paint their dreams,
A canvas wide, where sunlight beams.
Each stroke defies the silent norm,
In vibrant hues, they dare to form.

They dance on edges, cut with grace,
A heartbeat quickens, they find their place.
The brush in hand, they carve their way,
In fearless strokes, they greet the day.

Through shades of doubt, the artists glide,
With every layer, the truth inside.
In chaos found, they build their art,
A living tale, a beating heart.

They splash the skies with shades of hope,
A vivid world where dreams elope.
In every stroke, a story spun,
With brushes held, they have begun.

The gallery of life awaits,
Where audacity abates all fates.
Each canvas whispers tales anew,
In colors bold, they dare to pursue.

Chronicles of the Unwritten

In shadows deep, the tales unfold,
A parchment blank, wild dreams retold.
Whispers linger, secrets hum,
In pages blank, the future's drum.

The ink will flow, at dawn's first light,
With silent echoes, they take flight.
A world untouched, awaits the quill,
In every heart, a dream to fill.

The stories bloom like flowers rare,
In every line, a breath of air.
The unwritten whispers soft and low,
A journey waits, where few will go.

With courage sewn into the seams,
They stitch their hopes with fervent dreams.
Each stroke a promise, bold and bright,
In chronicles born of day and night.

They hold the pen, the world is cast,
In written dreams, the die is fast.
Every word a step anew,
In chronicles dressed in vibrant hue.

Starlit Paths of the Fearless

Beneath the sky of endless grace,
They walk the stars, they find their place.
With every step, the night ignites,
A trail of dreams, in silver lights.

The fearless hearts dare to explore,
Through cosmic seas, they yearn for more.
Each twinkling hope, a guiding flame,
In starlit paths, they stake their claim.

The universe sings with dreams so bright,
In endless realms, they chase the light.
Galaxies beckon, horizons call,
To wander forth, to dare, to fall.

In meteoric trails of promise made,
They carve their fate, where few have strayed.
The constellations wink and play,
In starlit dances, they find their way.

With every heartbeat, they embrace,
The vast unknown, a sacred space.
Together bound, they paint the skies,
In fearless journeys, they will rise.

Inventing Tomorrow's Tales

From ashes rise, new stories born,
In whispered dreams, a brand new morn.
With every thought, creation spins,
In realms unknown, the journey begins.

They spin the clock with hands of hope,
Inventing lives, where visions scope.
A tale unwritten, yet to unfold,
In daring hearts, the future's told.

The ink is fresh, the canvas bare,
With open minds, they cast their stare.
Tomorrow waits, a world anew,
In every heartbeat, they'll pursue.

Through trials faced, the fires ignite,
In shadows past, they seek the light.
With pens in hand, they break the mold,
In tales of courage, brave and bold.

Together woven, their dreams interlace,
Inventing futures, they find their place.
A tapestry rich, in colors bright,
Tomorrow's tales take wing in flight.

Stories Born from Challenge

In shadows deep, they rise and fight,
With every fall, they find their light.
Through trials fierce, their spirits soar,
From ashes lost, they seek for more.

A whispered hope in darkest night,
Each journey carved, a tale in sight.
With hearts ablaze, they write their fate,
Defying odds, they dare to wait.

The ink of grit, the pen of dreams,
With every tear, a stronger theme.
They weave their tales, both bold and bright,
From struggle's grip, they claim their right.

In tales of victory, truth prevails,
Against the storm, they ride the gales.
Each story shares a lesson learned,
In every page, a fire burned.

So let them tell, the world will see,
How challenges shape our destiny.
Through every wound, a scar that glows,
In stories born, the warrior shows.

Edges of the Possibility

On the brink where dreams collide,
A world awaits where hopes abide.
With whispered winds and open skies,
The edges call, where courage lies.

Step forth, the path is never clear,
With every doubt, ignite the cheer.
In woven threads of fate and chance,
Embrace the rhythm, join the dance.

Beyond the walls, the heart will lead,
Each leap of faith, a daring seed.
In lands unknown, adventure waits,
With wide-eyed wonder, it creates.

At every turn, the choice is yours,
To break the chains, to open doors.
For life's a canvas, bold and wide,
At edges drawn, let dreams reside.

So linger not where comfort stays,
Embrace the bold, ignite the blaze.
In endless realms where hopes can roam,
On edges found, you'll find your home.

Visions that Break Boundaries

In minds where colors intertwine,
Bold visions spark, a radiant sign.
With eyes that see beyond the veil,
They carve out paths, they blaze the trail.

Through whispers soft, ideas grow,
Defying limits, they overflow.
Inventive hearts refuse to yield,
With every thought, a new world healed.

With brush in hand and words that sing,
They build the dreams, the change they bring.
In every break, a chance to rise,
To see the world through clearer eyes.

For boundaries fade where passions meet,
United souls will not retreat.
In vibrant hues, each story shines,
As visions break, the future aligns.

So let the dreams take flight and soar,
In realms where hearts forever pour.
With courage fierce, and voices strong,
We'll sing the dreams where we belong.

The Melody of Resilience

In echoes soft, a song begins,
With every note, a tale it spins.
Through storms that rage and tempests howl,
Resilience blooms, an inner growl.

Each setback met, a worthy cause,
With steadfast hearts, they earn their applause.
In harmony, they rise anew,
A melody forged from battles true.

With whispered strength, they march ahead,
In rhythm found, they won't be led.
Through trials faced and mountains steep,
The melody sings, restoring deep.

In every quiet, thunder breaks,
A symphony that never shakes.
With every chord, the spirit gleams,
In resilience lies their brightest dreams.

So let them play, the song of fate,
With hearts aligned, they celebrate.
Through every struggle, lift your voice,
In melody, you find your choice.

Artistry in Defiance

With brush in hand, they paint the night,
Against the norm, they claim their right.
Colors clash in bold display,
An act of love, they find their way.

In shadows deep, the canvases breathe,
Stories told in every weave.
Sparks of passion, fierce and bright,
Artistry blooms in endless flight.

They dance with chaos, reject the rules,
Defying fate, they gather tools.
With every stroke, a world anew,
Unyielding hearts, their vision true.

In whispered tones, they urge the fight,
To see the world through different light.
The art that breaks, the art that bends,
In defiance, their spirit mends.

So let the colors sing and soar,
With every piece, they seek for more.
Artistry thrives where hope ignites,
In boundless realms, they claim their heights.

The Heart of a Risk-Taker

In the shadowed corners of chance's embrace,
Lies a heart that beats with an untamed grace.
Where courage stirs and doubts collide,
The thrill of life is their constant guide.

They leap from cliffs with open eyes,
In every fall, a chance to rise.
With every pulse, adventure calls,
And echoes deep within their walls.

Through storms of fear, they find their way,
In wild winds, they dance and sway.
The road less traveled, a daring flight,
For in the dark, they find their light.

With every step, they bend and break,
A tapestry of dreams they make.
A tapestry woven with threads of bold,
In every moment, a story told.

Their heart drums loud in the silent night,
A beacon bright, a guiding light.
Embrace the risk, the dance, the dare,
For life's a canvas, alive and rare.

Daring to Dream

In the still of dusk, a dream takes flight,
On wings of hope, it seeks the light.
With every heartbeat, it dares to soar,
A whisper soft, but held in core.

Through valleys deep, where shadows play,
Dreamers wander, come what may.
With visions bright, they paint the skies,
In every challenge, a new surprise.

Midnight wishes cast in stars,
Promises woven not too far.
With courage born from silent screams,
The daring souls revive their dreams.

They shatter chains, they break the mold,
In every story, they brave the cold.
A spark ignites amidst the gloom,
For in their hearts, the dreams still bloom.

So dare to dream, to chase the chase,
With every step, find your own space.
In wild embrace, take the leap,
For life's the treasure that you keep.

Whispers of the Unconventional

In quiet corners of a bustling town,
Ideas rise, where heads bow down.
A whisper soft, a gentle nudge,
Of paths untraveled, they won't judge.

With ink and quill, they craft their lore,
Against the tide, they seek for more.
Unfiltered thoughts, they hold in hand,
In lives unshackled, they take a stand.

The rules they break, the norms they bend,
With every glance, they will defend.
Against the current, they swim upstream,
In every heartbeat, an unconventional dream.

Through laughter light and shadows deep,
They find connections, secrets to keep.
In the unexpected, they find their spark,
In the whispers loud, they leave their mark.

So hear them sing in streets so wide,
With every note, let passion guide.
The unconventional, a gift to share,
In brilliant hues, they paint the air.

Colors Beyond the Norm

In the sky a hue of dreams,
Swirling bright with vibrant beams.
Fields of motion, colors play,
Dancing light in bold display.

Shadows whisper, secrets glow,
Tints of love in undertow.
Nature speaks in shades so rare,
A canvas brushed with tender care.

In twilight's grasp, the colors dive,
Radiant blushes, we come alive.
Mystic shades beckon the brave,
In every heart, they softly wave.

Echoes of a distant song,
Hues that weave where souls belong.
Awakening the artist's eye,
Colors call, they never lie.

Every stroke, a dream unleashed,
Beyond the norm, we are feasted.
Join the dance of vivid light,
In colors, find your true delight.

Unveiling the Hidden Muse

In shadows deep where whispers dwell,
The heart's pure voice, a secret spell.
An artist waits with bated breath,
To find the muse in life and death.

Through tangled thoughts and silent fears,
Emerges light to dry the tears.
A gentle nudge, a soul revealed,
The hidden spark, a bond concealed.

With every stroke, each word aligns,
Awakening the heart that shines.
Eager hands with passion claw,
Unveiling truth with every flaw.

Each gaze a door, each sigh a key,
Unlocking dreams where we can be.
In quiet moments, in the storm,
The muse reveals a heart reborn.

So let us dance through tangled lines,
Release the doubts, embrace the signs.
For in the shadow, light shall fuse,
A masterpiece, the hidden muse.

Embers of Aspiration

From ashes rise, the embers glow,
In every heart, a fire can grow.
Flickers of hope, they pierce the night,
Guiding us to dreams in flight.

Through storms we push, through trials we wade,
Each step we take, our fears will fade.
The sparks ignite the passion's blaze,
In the dark, we weave our ways.

With every breath, ambition calls,
Through leap of faith, we break the walls.
A vision born from radiant dust,
In the fire, we find our trust.

So gather 'round these glowing signs,
With every challenge, courage shines.
The embers whisper tales untold,
Of dreams pursued and hearts of gold.

In every flicker, rise anew,
Find strength in what we aim to do.
With embers bright, our souls entwine,
A blazing path, our spirits shine.

Voices Unbound

In echoes strong, our voices rise,
Resounding truth beneath the skies.
Each note a thread in woven sound,
We speak of love, our hearts unbound.

From silent depths, we lift our song,
Together we grow ever strong.
United in the joy and pain,
In every word, the world we gain.

In whispered fervor, hopes reclaim,
Timeless echoes, without shame.
Our voices danced in moonlit air,
Unbound and free, we boldly dare.

Through valleys low and mountains high,
We sing our truths, we will not lie.
Every heart that beats in time,
A chorus rich, a rhythmic rhyme.

So let us rise, together strive,
In harmony, our spirits thrive.
With voices joined, we'll break the ground,
In every heart, our dreams are found.

Legacy of the Boldhearted

In shadows deep where whispers dwell,
The stories of the brave do swell.
They carved a path, fierce and bright,
Their spirits soar, a guiding light.

With hearts ablaze and dreams in hand,
They forged their truths upon the land.
Through storm and strife, their voices rang,
In unity, they boldly sang.

Against the tides that sought to bind,
They sought the truth, no fear confined.
In every heartbeat, every breath,
They lived their lives, defying death.

The legacy of those we praise,
Is written in their fearless ways.
With every tale of brave endeavor,
Their spirit shines—a bond forever.

The Light of Audacious Moments

In fleeting time, we seize the bold,
Each moment shines, a tale retold.
With courage fierce and hearts afire,
We chase our dreams, we lift them higher.

The vibrant spark that fuels our fight,
Ignites the day, transforms the night.
In laughter shared and sighs of hope,
We find our way, our daring scope.

With every choice, we break the chain,
In daring steps, we feel no pain.
We stand as one, our spirits free,
In audacity, we find our glee.

Each challenge faced, a lesson learned,
In blazing paths, the tides are turned.
In every heartbeat, our story grows,
The light of moments boldly glows.

Sails of Unwavering Resolve

With winds that howl and waves that surge,
We raise our sails, we feel the urge.
Through tempests wild and calm so clear,
Our steadfast hearts shall steer us near.

Each crest we climb, each trough we brave,
In unity, we find our wave.
With resolute eyes, we chart our course,
In every struggle, we feel the force.

The horizon calls, a beacon bright,
We sail with purpose, fueled by light.
In distant shores, our dreams unfurl,
With unwavering hope, we greet the world.

Together strong, our spirits bound,
In oceans vast, our strength is found.
With every journey, our tale is told,
On sails of resolve, we shall be bold.

Breaking the Molds

In confines marked by ancient lore,
We dream of skies we've not explored.
In every heart, a restless spark,
That cries for change, ignites the dark.

With voices raised, we shatter glass,
Defy the norms, and boldly pass.
In unity, we craft the new,
With open hearts, we see it through.

The molds that bound us, cracked and worn,
With every step, our paths reborn.
In every silence, courage heard,
We write our fate without a word.

With hands that mold the future bright,
We sculpt our dreams under moonlight.
In every echo of our call,
We break the molds and rise for all.

Voices from the Edge

In twilight's grasp, whispers flow,
Silent truths we come to know.
On the fringe where shadows dwell,
Echoes call, a siren's bell.

Fears entwined in every breath,
Dancing close to dreams and death.
Yet in silence, courage stands,
Reaching out with open hands.

Through the noise, a gentle plea,
From the edge, we long to be free.
Hear the call, embrace the night,
In our hearts, a spark of light.

Voices rise like waves at sea,
Breaking chains, to truly be.
In the dark, the truth will swell,
A testament, our souls to tell.

Mirrors of Inner Strength

Reflecting shadows, strength ignites,
In stillness, find the inner fights.
Mirrors show what we conceal,
A warrior's heart, forever real.

In every crack, a story speaks,
With every tear, resilience peaks.
Through storms that shake the very core,
We rise anew, forevermore.

Hand in hand with trials faced,
In the fire, our fears are laced.
Yet from ashes, we emerge,
With every challenge, a new surge.

Gather strength from those who care,
In unity, we boldly dare.
Mirrors show what others see,
A tapestry of true unity.

Threads of Unrestrained Imagination

Woven dreams in vibrant hues,
Crafted tales that break the blues.
In our minds, worlds intertwine,
Infinite paths where wonders shine.

Threads extend to skies unknown,
Every thought, a seed is sown.
Through the fabric, visions drift,
Imagination, a precious gift.

Colors splatter, shapes collide,
In every heart, a universe wide.
Bound by nothing, soaring high,
On wings of dreams, we learn to fly.

With every stitch, a story's spun,
From quiet nights to blazing sun.
Threads of hope, forever strong,
In this realm, we all belong.

The Heart's Resilient Echo

Beneath the surface, whispers tread,
In the silence, the heart is led.
An echo of the battles fought,
In every heartbeat, lessons taught.

Through valleys low and mountains high,
The heart persists, a lullaby.
With every pulse, a tale unfolds,
Of love and loss, of courage bold.

In quiet moments, strength is found,
A melody, a life unbound.
Echoes ripple through the years,
Resilience blooms through all our fears.

The heart's song, a timeless tune,
Guiding stars beneath the moon.
In every echo, life transcends,
A symphony that never ends.

The Mosaic of Self-Discovery

In fragments bright, I seek my truth,
Each piece a whisper, a lost youth.
Through jagged edges, I find my grace,
Revealing stories in every space.

Colors blend in a vibrant hue,
Shaping visions of something new.
With every shard, I learn to see,
The art within this tapestry.

Old fears fade, replaced by light,
In the chaos, I ignite.
Each moment stitched, each heartbeat loud,
In this mosaic, I stand proud.

Reflecting back, I find my way,
In shadows cast by yesterday.
With courage grown, I piece it whole,
Embracing every part of soul.

The journey calls, a dance of years,
Through laughter, dreams, and quiet tears.
A masterpiece, forever forged,
In the mosaic, I am engorged.

Illuminated Hues of the Heart

Beneath the stars, my spirit glows,
With every beat, the passion flows.
In shades of love, I find my voice,
In every silence, I rejoice.

Soft whispers dance on evening air,
Awakening dreams without a care.
Brushstrokes bright on canvas wide,
Illuminated by love's tide.

Through every struggle, every sigh,
These hues of hope will never die.
With tender colors, I paint my fate,
In the gallery of love, no room for hate.

Blending moments, both dark and light,
A symphony plays through the night.
Each hue reflects a fleeting glance,
In this heartbeat, a wild romance.

So hold my hand through shadows cast,
In radiant colors, our love is vast.
With every stroke, our spirits fly,
In illuminated hues, we touch the sky.

Threads of Wild Inspiration

In whispers soft, ideas bloom,
Threads of gold weave through the gloom.
From nature's heart, the passion flows,
In tangled roots, the wildness grows.

Moments dance like flames in air,
Fleeting glimpses, bright and rare.
With each encounter, sparks ignite,
In chaos born, the soul takes flight.

The world alive, with colors rich,
In every challenge, we find a niche.
With every thread, our stories spin,
In the tapestry, we dive in.

Courage found in hearts so bold,
Every dream, a thread to hold.
In wild creation, we find our call,
Together we rise, together we fall.

Through stormy nights and sunlit days,
These threads unite in myriad ways.
In every moment, inspiration thrives,
A dance of threads, where passion drives.

A Journey Through Uncharted Waters

Beneath the waves, the unknown lies,
A canvas vast, beneath the skies.
Each ripple hints of tales untold,
In waters deep, adventures bold.

The currents pull, a wild embrace,
In search of dreams, I find my place.
With every stroke against the tide,
The journey calls; I cannot hide.

Stars above, our guides so bright,
Navigating through the night.
In every wave, a lesson learned,
In each wretched storm, I'm turned.

With a heart full of hope and fear,
I chart the course, the path is clear.
In uncharted waters, I find my home,
In the seas of courage, I freely roam.

For life's great voyage is never straight,
But swells of wonder and twists of fate.
Embracing chaos, the heart will soar,
Through uncharted waters, I seek for more.

Against the Grain of Caution

In shadows cast, the whispers sigh,
Dare to dance beneath the sky.
Embrace the thrill, resist the fear,
Let intuition steer you near.

With every step, the heart beats loud,
Breaking free from reason's shroud.
The roads less traveled call your name,
A fire ignites, an untamed flame.

In vibrant hues, the wild unfolds,
A narrative daring, brave, and bold.
Every risk, a story spun,
In the tapestry of life begun.

Let the tide of fate entwine,
In every moment, brightly shine.
Against the grain, the truest way,
To find your voice, to seize the day.

Realms of Inspired Potential

Awake within the quiet soul,
Existence whispers, making whole.
In dreams that soar on wings of light,
Embrace the dawn, a future bright.

Ideas dance where shadows lay,
Through trials faced, the heart finds sway.
In painted hues of vibrant thought,
A masterpiece of courage wrought.

With every spark, a new dawn breaks,
Awakening the world, it shakes.
In realms unseen, let visions flow,
The seeds of hope begin to grow.

Through pathways forged in passion's flame,
Each step we take, we stake our claim.
In stories told and journeys bold,
The potential within us unfolds.

Paintbrushes of the Soul

With every stroke, emotions rise,
Colors whisper, truths, and sighs.
In the canvas of our days,
Art reveals in myriad ways.

Hearts entwined in vibrant hue,
Layered stories come into view.
Through brushes light, we seek to tell,
The silent echoes, river's swell.

A splash of love, a hint of pain,
Moments captured, joy and strain.
Textures rich, in shadows deep,
A legacy that weaves, and keeps.

In art we find the purest form,
Breaking norms, challenging the norm.
With paintbrushes from deep within,
We craft the world where we begin.

The Ladder of Leap of Faith

Upward climbs the heart's desire,
Each rung a step, a spark, a fire.
With trembling hands and open mind,
What lies above is yet to find.

The whispers call from high above,
Where dreams converge and merge with love.
A leap should grace the heart's embrace,
To find the heights, we must face.

With courage firm, the spirit soars,
Every challenge opens doors.
In faith, we rise, against the doubt,
Transforming fears, erasing rout.

In every step, the strength we gain,
The ladder leads through joy and pain.
Trust the climb, embrace the view,
For in the leap, we find what's true.

Embarking on the Untraveled

In the dawn's soft light we stand,
With dreams like grains of sand.
Paths unknown lie before our eyes,
Hopes that reach beyond the skies.

Steps are taken, hearts will race,
Through the wild, we find our place.
Every twist, a story told,
Adventures waiting to unfold.

Mountains high, rivers deep,
Secrets in the shadows sleep.
Fear may whisper, strength will yell,
In this journey, all is well.

With each mile, we learn to trust,
In the path, a wanderer's dust.
Voices echo through the trees,
Guiding us with gentle ease.

So we tread, the road our friend,
Every moment, time to spend.
On the untraveled, dreams unwind,
In the journey, ourselves we find.

Sparks in the Darkness

When the night wraps all in gloom,
And shadows dance within the room.
A flicker glows, a silent fight,
Sparks of hope ignite the night.

In the depths where silence dwells,
A whisper breaks the hidden shells.
Every heart can find its flame,
Kindling courage, not the same.

Through the fog, a path appears,
Each step forward quells the fears.
Light will shine in darkest hours,
Love and grace, our guiding powers.

We gather strength from what we face,
Finding joy in each embrace.
Together we rise, hand in hand,
Creating warmth across the land.

In the chaos, still we stand,
Bound by dreams, a hopeful band.
Sparks in the dark, a beacon bright,
Together, we will chase the light.

The Unfolding Journey

Each moment breathes like a soft wind,
The pages turn, the story begins.
A tapestry of dreams we weave,
In the journey, we learn to believe.

Footsteps tracing paths of old,
Tales of courage waiting to be told.
With open hearts, we search for meaning,
In every moment, life's true gleaning.

Mountains, valleys, oceans wide,
On this journey, we learn to glide.
With every trial, we grow more strong,
Finding where our souls belong.

Wonders wait in the unseen,
In the silence, we hear the serene.
Each experience, a piece of our art,
Guiding us back to our heart.

So let us walk through every door,
Leave behind what came before.
In the unfolding, we find our cheer,
The journey's magic drawing near.

Voices that Challenge Silence

In the stillness where shadows loom,
Voices rise to break the gloom.
Words like rivers carving stone,
Bringing life to what was known.

With courage painted on their lips,
They gather strength, they rise, they grip.
Challenging the whispers, they demand,
To be heard across the land.

Every story, a battle won,
In the light of the shining sun.
Voices echoing through the night,
Awakening the lost to fight.

No longer bound by muted chains,
Every heart, a burning flame.
Together they sing, together they roar,
Breaking barriers, opening doors.

In this symphony of truth and grace,
The silence shatters, takes its place.
Voices that challenge, uplift, inspire,
Kindle in us a blazing fire.

Whispers of Boldness

In the night, a soft allure,
Calls to those who seek for more.
A voice that breaks the silent chains,
Boldly whispers, courage gains.

Each step forward, a tale unfolds,
With dreams ignited, hearts turned gold.
Fear fades away in daring light,
Boldness finds its way to flight.

Through shadows where the brave reside,
Whispers thrive, no need to hide.
With every heartbeat, a new spark,
Lighting up the once-dark park.

Let the winds of change now blow,
Carrying hope where rivers flow.
Embrace the leap, defy the fall,
Whispers guide us through it all.

In unity, our voices rise,
Boldness born beneath vast skies.
Together we will chase the dawn,
In whispers, we are never gone.

The Colors of Fearlessness

In vibrant hues, the brave arise,
Drenching fears in painted skies.
With strokes of courage, they create,
A world where doubt cannot dictate.

Crimson for the fires within,
Amber glow of steadfast grin.
Emerald dreams set wild and free,
Colors blend in harmony.

Golden threads of hope entwine,
Beneath the stars, our spirits shine.
Shade of lavender, calm the storm,
Fearless hearts begin to swarm.

From shadows to the open light,
Colors flash, a vibrant sight.
With every brush, a vision clear,
In fearlessness, we conquer fear.

Embrace the palette, paint it bold,
Unwavering, let stories unfold.
In every hue, a tale of worth,
Fearlessness blooms upon this earth.

Daring to Dream Beyond

In whispers soft, dreams take flight,
Beyond the known, into the light.
A spark ignites from depths untold,
Daring hearts brave, fierce and bold.

Through veils of doubt, hope will weave,
Boundless worlds for us to cleave.
With every thought, new paths appear,
Daring to dream, we shift the sphere.

Hold tight to visions, bright and grand,
In our grasp, the future stands.
Building bridges, we shall explore,
Daring to dream, forevermore.

With every step, horizons grow,
Cultivating seeds we sow.
The tapestry of life unfolds,
Daring souls, let stories told.

Together we shall chase the stars,
With hearts wide open, free from bars.
In dreams, we find the strength to see,
Daring to dream, our spirits free.

Heartbeats of Risk

Within the pulse, adventure hums,
A rhythm whispers, daring drums.
With every beat, the brave ignite,
Heartbeats of risk, taking flight.

The dance of fate, uncertain paths,
In risk, we find what truly lasts.
With open hearts, we venture forth,
Charting lands of endless worth.

In moments fleeting, we embrace,
The thrill of life, a wild race.
Every heartbeat, a choice we make,
Risk beckons us, we shan't forsake.

With courage stitched in every seam,
Paths untraveled, we must redeem.
As heartbeats echo, clear and true,
Risk whispers softly, guiding you.

Embrace the chance, let fears unwind,
In heartbeats of risk, treasures find.
Through valleys low and mountains high,
Life is lived where risks comply.

A Tapestry of the Unwritten

In shadows deep, tales await,
Whispers woven from fate.
Threads of dreams pull tight and strong,
Binding silence to a song.

Colors blend, a rich delight,
Stories dance, both day and night.
Each strand bears a hidden truth,
A tapestry spun from youth.

The loom of life, ever unfurling,
In secret corners, stories twirling.
Imagined worlds yet to be drawn,
In heartbeats echo, now and dawn.

Voices call from distant shores,
Unwritten lines, behind closed doors.
With gentle hands, we stitch anew,
In every thread, a vibrant hue.

When Stars Align in Courage

Beneath the night, fierce hearts emerge,
In shadows cast, we'll not diverge.
When stars align, we make our stand,
Together strong, a fearless band.

Through storms that howl and doubts that creep,
We find the strength our souls can keep.
Each spark ignites a burning flame,
In unity, we share the name.

With each step forward, fears do fade,
In courage found, true paths are laid.
We rise as one, our spirits bold,
In stories shared, our fate unfolds.

So lift your voice to skies above,
With open hearts and boundless love.
For when we stand, the world will see,
The power born in unity.

Fragments of a Brave Heart

In pieces scattered, yet so bright,
Each fragment holds a spark of light.
Brave hearts beat in wild embrace,
Daring paths we dare to trace.

With broken shards, we build anew,
In every crack, the light shines through.
Resilient souls, we rise once more,
In stormy seas, we seek the shore.

Each piece a story, deep and true,
Of battles fought and victories due.
Heroes lie in quiet fight,
With every tear, we claim our right.

So gather fragments, piece by piece,
In every hurt, we find release.
Together strong, we heal the part,
Creating beauty from a brave heart.

The Journey of the Unseen

In whispers soft, the journey starts,
Where unseen paths call to our hearts.
Each step we take, a secret found,
On winding roads, our souls unbound.

In stillness rare, we find our way,
Through shadows stretching, light will play.
With every turn, a lesson learned,
In silence deep, our spirits churned.

The way is long, yet full of grace,
In hidden depths, we find our place.
In dreams unspoken, hopes ignite,
The journey glows, a source of light.

So take a breath, embrace the mist,
In every moment, there's a twist.
The unseen guides us through the night,
In journeys shared, we find our light.

Soaring Beyond Limits

Beneath the wide and open skies,
A spirit yearns, it dares to rise.
With wings of courage, bold and bright,
It chases dreams, ignites the night.

Mountains high, and rivers deep,
Where shadows fall, we take our leap.
A whisper calls from far above,
In every heartbeat, lies the love.

Through storms we dance, we twist and sway,
Each gust of wind marks our way.
With laughter loud, we greet the dawn,
And in our flight, we'll carry on.

Unbound by fears, we twirl and spin,
In harmony, we find our win.
For in the sky, our hopes ascend,
Together, as we dare to blend.

So let the world, with all its weight,
Encourage us to challenge fate.
For soaring high is not confined,
In every soul, the brave we find.

The Art of Breaking Molds

In every shape, a story lies,
Yet bends the truth, distorts the skies.
With hammer strikes and fires anew,
We mold the world with every hue.

Society's chains, they shift and break,
From rigid paths, we choose to wake.
With every step, unique and free,
We craft the art of who we'll be.

Embrace the chaos, let it flow,
In vibrant waves, our visions grow.
A dance of colors, bold and grand,
We paint the dreams we understand.

They say it's wrong, they draw their lines,
But we are stars, in our designs.
To shatter glass, we rise as one,
Our journey's wild, we have begun.

For in our hearts, the fire ignites,
We venture forth to claim our rights.
The art of breaking molds is pure,
Together strong, we will endure.

Echoes of the Fearless Heart

In silent nights, our whispers call,
A bond that binds, it conquers all.
With every beat, the world awakes,
In fearless hearts, the courage stokes.

Through trials faced, we learn to strive,
Resilience grows, we come alive.
With every pulse, we brave the dark,
For hope ignites the fervent spark.

Together built, with dreams aligned,
In unity, our strength combined.
The echoes ring, through valleys vast,
In moments shared, a shadow cast.

For courage flows in every vein,
It sings of love, it conquers pain.
And in the echoes, we shall find,
The fervor born from hearts unlined.

So let us rise, our voices clear,
With fearless hearts, we have no fear.
As echoes dance in moonlit night,
We stand as one, and share the light.

Brushstrokes of Resistance

In colors fierce, our truths unfold,
Each brushstroke strong, a tale retold.
With hands that forge, the canvas bends,
In art we find the strength to mend.

With every hue, we paint our fight,
From shadows cast, we claim the light.
Resilient spirits break the mold,
As stories bright, in strokes, behold.

Bold lines define our will to stand,
In unity, we raise our hand.
Against the tides that seek to drown,
Through vibrant art, we wear our crown.

For every stroke that breaks the dark,
A flame ignites, igniting spark.
With passion fierce, and voices sound,
In brushstrokes deep, our hearts are found.

So let us rise with colors bright,
And join the dance of day and night.
Through art, we'll pave our way, persist,
In every canvas, we resist.

Horizons in Uncharted Waters

Waves break gently on the shore,
Secrets hidden in the core,
Sails unfurl to catch the breeze,
Adventures call upon the seas.

With every star, a path we trace,
Guided by the moon's embrace,
Anchors lifted, spirits soar,
New horizons we explore.

Currents strong, they pull us near,
Yet we face the void, no fear,
Fishes dance in depths below,
In these waters, we will grow.

Storms will rage and skies will cry,
Through the chaos, we will fly,
Braving tempests, forged and free,
Life's adventure, meant to be.

Every journey has its tale,
With each whisper of the gale,
Horizons beckon, dreams in sight,
In uncharted waters, we ignite.

Threads of Unshackled Thought

In shadows deep where whispers dwell,
Ideas bloom, like a secret spell,
Each thread woven with careful grace,
Unshackled minds, we find our place.

Colors splash on canvas wide,
Imagination opens wide,
Voices rise, no chains to bind,
Creative sparks ignite the mind.

Words take flight, like birds in sky,
Fluttering low, then soaring high,
Every thought a dance, a song,
Threads of freedom, where we belong.

In the realm of endless dreams,
Reality is not what it seems,
Courage fuels our quest for more,
Unlocking futures at the door.

Embrace the chaos, craft the art,
Feel the rhythm, hear the heart,
From shackles gone, we take our stand,
Threads whisper truths, hand in hand.

Beyond the Dull and Dreary

Through the fog, a light appears,
Chasing shadows, calming fears,
Colors brighten, spirits lift,
In the mundane, we find the gift.

Moments glisten like dewdrops rare,
Beneath the weight, we learn to care,
Life's palette rich, we paint anew,
Beyond the dull, a vibrant view.

Dreams awaken, hearts ignite,
In the darkness, we find light,
Each step forward, a new chance,
To break the silence with a dance.

The ordinary turns profound,
In the stillness, joy is found,
Beyond the dreary, skies expand,
With open hearts, we take a stand.

Hope unfurls its gentle guise,
In the mundane, beauty lies,
Beyond the dull, we rise to see,
The magic blooms, the soul's decree.

Battlegrounds of Imagination

In the mind's eye, battles wage,
Where thoughts collide and dreams engage,
Colors clash and shadows fight,
In the realm of endless night.

Heroes rise with courage bold,
Stories break, yet to be told,
Every twist, a chance to grow,
In this space, our visions flow.

Victory tastes like sweet delight,
In the clash of dark and light,
A dance of destinies entwined,
In the chaos, peace we find.

Upon the fields where visions soar,
Art is weapon, heart's rapport,
Imagined worlds ignite the flame,
Battlegrounds of the wildest name.

And when the dust begins to clear,
New landscapes rise, we hold them dear,
For in this fight, we learn to see,
The power of creativity.

Shadows of the Unseen

In twilight's grasp, they softly creep,
Silent whispers, secrets deep.
The moonlight's dance, a gentle tease,
In shadows cast, our fears appease.

Beneath the veil, where dreams persist,
Flickering hopes, in twilight kissed.
Serpentine trails, where shadows glide,
They linger still, where we abide.

Echoes of thoughts, in corners hide,
In silent rooms, where whispers bide.
Figures loom, yet none are there,
In unseen worlds, we find our lair.

Stories woven, in fabric bright,
In every pause, a latent light.
The unseen hands, they shape our fate,
In shadowed corners, we contemplate.

A journey through the night's embrace,
In quietude, we find our space.
For shadows hold, what light can't see,
The unseen truth, setting us free.

Wings of Imagination

Upward we soar on thoughts unfurled,
To realms of dreams, a boundless world.
Colors bleed in the vivid sky,
On wings of hope, we dare to fly.

With every stroke, new visions form,
In gentle breezes, we ride the storm.
Dreams take flight, unchained and bold,
In whispered paths, our hearts consoled.

Through forests thick and oceans wide,
We seek the wonders that worlds provide.
Imagination's spark, it brightly glows,
Leading us where the wild wind blows.

In silence deep, creation sings,
As we embrace what magic brings.
With every thought, our spirits rise,
On airy wings, we touch the skies.

Together we dance, across the night,
In every shadow, the urge for light.
Oh, let us dream, let hearts take flight,
For wings of imagination shine so bright.

Ascent to the Unmapped

Beyond the borders, horizons gleam,
In uncharted lands, we chase our dream.
With every step, the ground transforms,
An ascent to places where passion warms.

Mountains call with voices clear,
In whispers soft, they draw us near.
Scaling heights where few have tread,
In the silence, our fears shed.

Paths unknown, through mist and haze,
We navigate the winding maze.
With compass hearts, we journey on,
In every challenge, we find the dawn.

Stars above like lanterns guide,
In the night, our hopes abide.
Odyssey bold, a tale to share,
As we rise from earth to air.

In every stumble, lessons learned,
For each new quest, the spirit yearned.
Ascent to the unmapped, here we stand,
With open hearts, we claim the land.

A Symphony of Inner Radiance

In silent chords, the heart does play,
A melody bright, to light the way.
Notes of joy in stillness bloom,
Creating warmth in shadowed room.

With every breath, the harmonies swell,
Echoes of peace in the soul's citadel.
Strings of hope, with whispers ignite,
A symphony born from depths of night.

Graceful movements, like waves on the shore,
Resonating deep, we long for more.
In music's arms, we find our grace,
A dance of life, a sacred space.

From inner wells, the radiance flows,
Illuminating paths that memory knows.
In every heartbeat, the rhythm divine,
A symphony crafted, in love's design.

Together we rise, in song and light,
With unity found, we take our flight.
A chorus of souls, forever entwined,
In a symphony of radiance, we shine.

The Canvas of the Intrepid

With brushes bold and colors bright,
They paint their dreams, chase the light.
Fearless hearts in every stroke,
Creating worlds, where spirits woke.

The canvas stretches wide and free,
A tapestry of possibility.
Each hue a tale, each shade a song,
In this vast realm, they all belong.

With every splash, they break the mold,
Adventures crafted, brave and bold.
The intrepid souls, they know no end,
In art's embrace, their hearts transcend.

Through swirling hues and vivid forms,
They weather every storm that warms.
Each masterpiece a silent roar,
Revealing truths behind each door.

So step into this vibrant space,
Where courage dwells and dreams embrace.
The canvas waits for you to start,
Unfold your story, share your heart.

Hand in Hand with Possibility

Two souls united, hands entwined,
In this embrace, their paths aligned.
With every step, the future glows,
A dance of hopes, where love bestows.

Together they climb mountains high,
Beneath the vast and endless sky.
With whispered dreams, they chart the way,
Hand in hand, come what may.

Each heartbeat echoes a new start,
Building bridges, mending hearts.
Through storms and sun, they find their grace,
In every moment, they find their place.

As seasons change, they grow and learn,
Embracing paths that twist and turn.
The world unfolds with every choice,
In perfect harmony, they rejoice.

With open minds, they chase the dawn,
In fearless love, they carry on.
Together they write their story bold,
Hand in hand, their dreams unfold.

Threads of the Unconventional

In a tapestry of vibrant threads,
They weave the tales that life embeds.
With colors strange and patterns wild,
The spirit of the free-formed child.

Each twist and turn a story told,
Of laughter, tears, and dreams grown old.
Unconventional paths that lead to grace,
Daring the world to embrace their space.

With needle sharp and vision clear,
They stitch together joy and fear.
The fabric rich, the edges frayed,
A masterpiece in every shade.

Beneath the norms, they carve their way,
Creating change, come what may.
The threads entwined, a vibrant blend,
In each connection, they transcend.

So gather 'round this woven art,
Feel the rhythm, hear the heart.
In every thread, a voice stands tall,
Together united, they shall not fall.

Beyond the Horizon of Tradition

Across the past, the future calls,
Beyond the borders, breaking walls.
With courage found in open minds,
They seek the truth that freedom finds.

Tradition whispers ancient tales,
Yet fresh ideas set the sails.
With every step, they redefine,
The pathways where their hearts entwine.

Through shadows cast by years gone by,
They chase the dreams that soar and fly.
Each sunset brings a brand new dawn,
A world reborn, paths drawn upon.

In dialogue of hearts combined,
The past and present intertwined.
With hands outstretched, they brave the night,
Embracing all that feels so right.

So venture forth, embrace the change,
In every moment, feel the range.
Beyond tradition, hearts can gleam,
In the horizon lies a dream.

The Joy of Taking Flight

With wings unfurled, I rise so high,
The winds embrace, I touch the sky.
Each gust a song, each turn a dance,
In this vast world, I take my chance.

The clouds below, so soft, so white,
I glide above, in pure delight.
A heart set free, no chains in sight,
In this moment, all feels right.

From heights, I see the beauty spread,
The earth below, in colors dressed.
With every beat, my spirit sings,
Embracing all that freedom brings.

The sun will sink, the day will fade,
Yet on these wings, I'm unafraid.
For in the dark, I find my guide,
A thousand stars, my heart's delight.

So let me soar, let me ignite,
This joy I feel when taking flight.
Forever bound to the wide blue sea,
In every leap, I find the free.

Fluttering between Fear and Freedom

In shadows cast, my heart does race,
Between the dark and open space.
A whispered doubt, a hope now glows,
In fragile dreams, my spirit grows.

The edge of fear, a tempting brink,
Yet in the void, my thoughts will sink.
I take a breath, I stand my ground,
In this tightrope, no glance around.

I feel the push, the pull, the sway,
In every choice, I find my way.
Each fluttered wing, each closing door,
A storm within that wants to soar.

Yet what is held in trembling hands?
The freedom blooms as courage stands.
With every doubt, a chance to fly,
Embracing up, refusing to hide.

For in this dance, I crave the light,
To bridge the gap from fear to flight.
And in that space, my heart beats true,
A world awaits, and I break through.

Bridging the Known and Unknown

A path divides, the old and new,
I take a step to wander through.
With every beat, the silence calls,
Into the depths where mystery falls.

The comfort lies in what I know,
Yet thrill ignites when I let go.
To dance upon the edge of fate,
And feel alive, I cannot wait.

The bridge it sways, yet strong it stands,
My heart in tune with unknown lands.
In twilight's glow, I make my mark,
Navigating shadows, sparked by dark.

Each step I take, a chance revealed,
In every choice, my fate is sealed.
The known is safe, the unknown's wild,
In both I find the heart of a child.

So here I stand, a soul reborn,
With dreamer's eyes, the night is worn.
For on this bridge, I choose to roam,
Bridging worlds, I find my home.

Unfurling the Canvas of Life

Brush strokes bright, colors entwine,
Dreams take flight, visions align.
Each hue a story, each shade a sigh,
On this canvas, moments fly.

With every stroke, we grit and weave,
Wonders arise, we choose to believe.
In shadows deep, light finds a way,
Unfurling life, come what may.

Textures pulse, emotions bold,
Layers of dreams, whispers unfold.
Time stands still, yet flows as we grow,
The canvas of life, forever aglow.

Crafting a tale with heart and soul,
Each splash of paint, making us whole.
Together we dance, we create, we try,
Unfurling the canvas, reaching the sky.

We paint our fears, we paint our grace,
Each brush stroke a step, each line a trace.
In this masterpiece, we learn and thrive,
With colors shared, we come alive.

Echoes of Untamed Spirit

Whispers of wind through the trees,
Calling us forth, setting us free.
Wild hearts roar, no chains to bind,
In echoes of spirit, dreams unwind.

With every heartbeat, let us run,
Chasing the stars, embracing the sun.
We dance through fields, untamed and bare,
In every echo, a life to share.

Mountains bow to the untold fire,
In courage, we rise, to reach higher.
The pulse of the earth, our rhythm and rhyme,
In echoes of spirit, we transcend time.

Nature's embrace, wild and true,
In its symphony, we find our due.
With souls entwined, let the boundaries break,
Echoes of spirit, for freedom's sake.

In the horizon where dreams ignite,
We write our stories, bold and bright.
Together we soar, forever we'll sing,
In the echoes of life, our spirits take wing.

Dancing in the Firelight

Flames flicker bright, shadows sway,
In firelight's glow, we find our way.
Laughter mingles with the night air,
Dancing souls, free without care.

Gathered close, hearts intertwined,
In the warmth of flames, true joy we find.
Rhythms of night guide our feet,
In this moment, our lives repeat.

Stories unfold with crackling sound,
In every ember, history found.
Joy and sorrow blend and ignite,
Dancing together in pure delight.

With every twirl, our spirits rise,
Under starlit blankets, beneath wide skies.
The fire whispers secrets untold,
As we lose ourselves in the warmth of gold.

Time stands still, wrapped in this glow,
In the firelight's dance, our spirits flow.
Together we weave a tapestry bright,
In the embrace of a magical night.

The Art of Brave Beginnings

With every dawn, new moments start,
The art of beginnings, a courageous heart.
Stepping forward, leaving the past,
Embracing the change, holding it fast.

A blank page waits, stories to tell,
In every heartbeat, we rise and fell.
With dreams as our brush, we paint the day,
The art of beginnings, in every sway.

Courage blooms in the face of dread,
In whispers of hope, our fears are shed.
With every choice, our path aligns,
Writing our tale, as fate entwines.

The canvas of life beckons anew,
Each stroke significant, brave and true.
In the journey ahead, we find our song,
The art of brave beginnings, where we belong.

So here's to the leaps, the risks that we take,
In the heart of beginnings, we learn to awake.
With open arms, let's welcome the night,
The art of beginnings, our future in sight.

Trailblazers of Thought

In shadows deep, they tread alone,
With minds ablaze, from stone to stone.
Ideas bloom in fertile ground,
Where silence drapes, a secret sound.

They question norms, they break the mold,
With every whisper, visions bold.
The daring hearts refuse to yield,
In gardens rich, their fate is sealed.

Through winding paths, the daring dance,
With every step, they seize the chance.
In corridors of uncharted dreams,
They weave the fabric of their themes.

With passion's flame, they light the way,
Unraveling truths that softly sway.
In minds ignited, the world ignites,
A force of wonder, pure delight.

Across the seas of vast unknown,
They sail with courage, seeds are sown.
In every thought that dares to rise,
A trail is blazed beneath the skies.

The Fire Within

Deep in the soul, a fire burns bright,
Fueling the dreams that soar in flight.
With every spark, potential grows,
Igniting passion, the heart knows.

Through darkest nights, the flames will dance,
Challenging fears, they take their stance.
With whispered hopes, the embers swell,
A beacon shines, tales they tell.

In moments still, when silence reigns,
The fire within breaks those chains.
Each flicker speaks of paths untold,
In warmth of love, the brave unfold.

As shadows pass, the glow persists,
A guiding light, the heart insists.
Through trials faced, the fire stays,
Forever bright in endless ways.

For every soul that dares to dream,
The fire within ignites the theme.
Resilient hearts will always find,
A way to soar, the path aligned.

Greater than the Ordinary

In every corner, life reveals,
A tale of strength, a heart that heals.
From mundane streets to skies so wide,
Adventures wait, the soul's true guide.

With eyes that see beyond the haze,
They wander through the quiet maze.
In fleeting moments, magic found,
Beneath the stars, their spirits bound.

They seek the beauty, raw and real,
A gentle touch, the warmth they feel.
With every breath, they rise and climb,
Transforming hours, bending time.

Greater than fate, they seize the day,
In every choice, a bold display.
In tender gestures, joy ignites,
Inviting hopes, illuminating sights.

In ordinary steps, they soar,
With every heartbeat, craving more.
For life is rich, and dreams take wing,
In every moment, our souls sing.

Chasing Daring Visions

With open hearts, they chase the light,
Daring visions that shine so bright.
Through hills and valleys, they stride bold,
In every whisper, dreams unfold.

The canvas wide, imagination flows,
As colors blend, potential grows.
They paint their truths across the sky,
In hues of hope, they aim to fly.

With every heartbeat, purpose found,
In every moment, love surrounds.
Through trials faced, they press ahead,
In daring paths where angels tread.

They rise with dawn, unafraid to roam,
For every step, they sculpt a home.
In visions bright, their spirits free,
They chase the daring, endlessly.

United in dreams, they cast their fate,
In every heartbeat, they create.
For visions bold are worth the chase,
Embracing life, in every space.

Whirlwinds of Originality

In the breeze of thought, ideas fly,
Twisting and turning, reaching the sky.
Colors collide in a vibrant dance,
Chasing the shadows, seizing the chance.

A spark ignites in the depths of the mind,
Revealing treasures that we may find.
Like swirling leaves in autumn's embrace,
Original visions begin to take place.

With every whirl, a new tune is sung,
Crafted from whispers of hearts that are young.
They spin and twirl in a ceaseless spree,
In the whirlwind of thought, we are truly free.

A mosaic of dreams painted in air,
Each piece distinct, yet beyond compare.
Together they form a breathtaking view,
In the whirlwind of originality, we renew.

Paint Splashes in the Shadow

In corners dim, where color hides,
A brush held firm, the canvas bides.
With every splash, the darkness quakes,
A story born, with every stroke it makes.

Silhouettes dance, a vibrant tease,
Vivid forms, like whispers in trees.
Life is captured in hues so bold,
Where shadows linger, new tales unfold.

Each drop of paint tells tales untold,
In the heart of night, where dreams unfold.
Creating worlds, both wild and grand,
In the quiet of shadows, we take a stand.

With chaos reigned, and colors that clash,
A symphony formed in a glorious flash.
In the shelter of darkness, a vision to show,
Paint splashes bright in the ebb of the glow.

A Legacy of the Unique

From whispers of time, a legacy bound,
In stories woven, the lost are found.
Each thread distinct, in a tapestry bright,
We are the echoes of their light.

With footsteps that wander through fields of dreams,
Every voice whispers, or so it seems.
Carved in the hearts of those who dare,
A legacy blooms in the softest air.

In laughter shared and tears that flow,
A unique tale we each bestow.
Together we rise, apart we shine,
In a world where uniqueness intertwines.

For every soul is a story spun,
Crafted and cherished, never outdone.
Against the tide, we long to seek,
To embrace our truth, and sing our unique.

Crafting with Uncommon Belief

In the forge of will, dreams take their flight,
With hands that shape the softest light.
Every vision formed, a promise to keep,
Crafting with care, the soul's heart deep.

With every heartbeat, a new seed we sow,
In the garden of thought where ideas grow.
Nurturing dreams, with tender finesse,
Creating a world, in its truest dress.

Uncommon belief fuels the fire within,
With courage to stand, where others begin.
Colors and textures, a vivid embrace,
Crafting our journeys, with style and grace.

In the act of creation, unity sings,
From the heart emerges the joy that it brings.
With every stroke, the spirit takes flight,
Crafting a moment, in the depth of the night.

Embracing the Unknown

In shadows deep, we glimpse the light,
A world unwritten, fears take flight.
With every step, new paths we find,
In the heart's whisper, we're intertwined.

The stars align, we take a chance,
In the silent night, we begin to dance.
Each heartbeat echoes a call so clear,
The unknown's embrace holds no fear.

A journey starts with a single thought,
Lessons learned, battles fought.
In courage found, we rise anew,
Together we stand, with skies so blue.

Let go of doubts, let dreams take wing,
In every ending, new beginnings spring.
With open hearts, through storms we glide,
In the unknown, we shall reside.

What lies ahead, no one can tell,
But in the pursuit, we weave our spell.
Embracing life, come what may,
In the unknown, we find our way.

The Spark of Daring Innovation

A flicker bright in minds so bold,
Ideas stir, daring to unfold.
From dreams ignited, new paths arise,
In the realm of thought, the future lies.

Crafting visions with hands of light,
Building bridges to the night.
In every failure, lessons gleaned,
A tapestry of hopes and dreams.

Collaboration fuels the fire,
Together we climb, ever higher.
With passion's breath, we push the bounds,
In every heartbeat, innovation sounds.

Challenging norms, we break the mold,
Through risks we take, our stories told.
In curiosity's dance, we find our place,
The spark of daring in every face.

Inventing futures, as dreams collide,
With daring hearts, we turn the tide.
Together we rise, ignite the flame,
In the world of change, we stake our claim.

From whispers soft to thunderous roars,
In every heartbeat, innovation soars.
Boundless visions of what can be,
The spark of daring, forever free.

Beyond the Horizon of Possibility

Beneath the vast and endless sky,
We seek a place where dreams can fly.
Beyond the horizon, fate does wait,
With open arms and a heart so great.

In every whisper, a promise lies,
With courage as wings, we will rise.
Through valleys low and mountains tall,
We venture forth, heeding the call.

The journey winds like rivers flow,
Through trials faced, our spirits grow.
In the distance gleams a guiding star,
Beyond the horizon, we travel far.

With eyes wide open, we chase the dawn,
Each moment cherished, never withdrawn.
In unity's strength, we dare to dream,
Together we forge this vibrant theme.

What awaits us, we cannot know,
But bold we march, where wild winds blow.
Each heartbeat pulses with endless grace,
Beyond the horizon, we find our place.

In every sunset, a new light beams,
Beyond the horizon, we live our dreams.
With hope as our anchor, we sail the sea,
To realms unknown, where we are free.

The Vibrancy of Unchecked Dreams

In the quiet corners of the mind,
Unchecked dreams, so rare to find.
Colors burst, igniting the night,
In each heart's whisper, pure delight.

A canvas blank, invites our art,
Every stroke, a brand new start.
Imaginations soar on wings so wide,
In a world of wonder, joy can't hide.

With laughter bright, and voices clear,
We shatter silence, cast aside fear.
The vibrancy flows, a river wide,
In the heart's pulse, dreams don't divide.

Through swirling thoughts, we dance and weave,
In this tapestry, we believe.
Each thread a story, strong and true,
In the vibrancy, we find the new.

Let passions rise, let spirits soar,
In the world of dreams, we're hungry for more.
With every heartbeat, life ignites,
In unchecked dreams, we seek the heights.

A kaleidoscope of hope and grace,
In every moment, we embrace space.
Vibrant visions dance in the stream,
In the fabric of life, we chase the dream.

Wings of the Unexplored

In shadows where the silence dwells,
The whispers call from distant wells.
With every beat, the heart takes flight,
To chase the dreams that kiss the night.

Each path unfolds like pages new,
Through valleys deep, 'neath skies so blue.
Adventure beckons with a glow,
In realms where only spirits go.

The winds, they swirl like tales untold,
Embrace the brave, the seekers bold.
From heights above, the view expands,
A tapestry of distant lands.

With courage forged from hopes alight,
We rise like stars, igniting night.
In every heartbeat, every scream,
We soar beyond what others dream.

So spread your wings, let wild hearts soar,
For life awaits with open door.
In unknown skies let spirits play,
In wings of gold, we find our way.

Banners of Boldness

In fields of courage, banners fly,
Reflecting strength that dares to try.
Where dreams are sown like seeds of fire,
Each heart a flame, each hope a choir.

Stand tall, embrace the stormy skies,
Let not the fear of failure rise.
Carve your name in every stone,
With every step, you stand alone.

A tapestry of choice unspooled,
In the face of doubts, we are fueled.
With hearts ablaze, we sing our song,
Defiant souls who long belong.

In every whisper, every shout,
In shadows deep, erase the doubt.
Boldness breeds in darkest night,
A brighter day is born from fight.

So wave your banners, let them fly,
With colors loud against the sky.
Each fear faced is a tale retold,
In pursuit of dreams, be ever bold.

Vignettes of the Untamed

In forests wild where spirits roam,
The stories rise, they find a home.
Each whisper carried by the breeze,
A fragment of the ancient trees.

In fleeting moments, time stands still,
A glimpse of nature's rugged thrill.
The brush of grass beneath the sun,
Reminds us all how life can run.

With every glance, a story weaves,
In shadows deep, the heart believes.
Through tangled roots and mountain air,
We gather tales, our souls laid bare.

Each sunset paints a canvas wide,
Where colors blend, and dreams collide.
In every heartbeat, echoes roam,
The wild within, forever home.

So breathe it in, the untamed call,
In nature's grasp, we find the all.
In moments pure and wild, we thrive,
In vignettes crafted, we come alive.

Tides of Transformation

With rising tides, the world does change,
In waves of time, we feel the range.
Through every ebb and flowing crest,
We find the strength to face our quest.

The moon, it pulls the sea to dance,
In every chance, our spirits prance.
With courage found in shifting sands,
We shape our fate with willing hands.

Each ripple tells a tale anew,
Of battles fought and visions true.
In depths unknown, we search for light,
To guide us through the darkest night.

Transformed by storms, we rise and bend,
Each struggle faced, a chance to mend.
Like oceans vast, our hearts expand,
In tides of change, we make our stand.

So ride the waves, let currents steer,
In every change, embrace the fear.
With shifting tides comes endless chance,
In transformation, life's sweet dance.

Echoing Unseen Heights

In the stillness where whispers dwell,
Voices rise, like a secret spell.
Wings unfurl, in the quiet might,
Chasing shadows into the light.

Mountains call, though silence shrouds,
Every heartbeat, echoing loud.
Dreams take flight, above the trees,
In unseen heights, where souls find ease.

A soft breeze carries tales untold,
Of ancient paths and hearts so bold.
The sky stretches, vast and wide,
While echoes of the past abide.

Nature's hands weave threads of fate,
In harmony, we resonate.
With every step, we hear the song,
A tapestry where we belong.

Together, we rise, hand in hand,
On echoes built from dreams so grand.
These unseen heights, we climb as one,
Underneath the watchful sun.

Foraging New Frontiers

In the wild where whispers roam,
Adventures call, far from home.
Gathering strength in every stride,
Across the fields, where hopes abide.

New frontiers, a daring quest,
In the echoes, we've been blessed.
Through fields of uncertainty, we tread,
With hearts ablaze and minds widespread.

Paths unfurl as dawn awakes,
Treading softly, the earth quakes.
With curious eyes, we seek and find,
Treasures lost to the weary mind.

Foraging dreams in open skies,
Where possibilities surely rise.
Every step a story told,
In the hands of the brave and bold.

Together we stand, side by side,
With courage as our steadfast guide.
These new frontiers, we shall explore,
With hearts ignited, forevermore.

The Courageous Quill

In realms of ink where muses play,
A quill takes flight, the words convey.
From shadows deep, to vibrant light,
Weaving tales through day and night.

With every stroke, a dream defined,
In parchment's grace, our truths aligned.
The ink flows strong, a river's might,
Giving voice to the heart's delight.

Courage blooms in written lines,
Revealing paths where fate entwines.
A saga carved in fleeting time,
The quill dances, pure and sublime.

Through stormy seas and quiet lands,
Crafting worlds with trembling hands.
In silent corners, the whispers swell,
Invoking magic, the courageous quill.

Let words ignite, let passion soar,
With every line, we seek for more.
In narratives bold, we find our call,
With courage, we rise, we dare, we fall.

Pulse of the Fearless Artist

In vibrant strokes and colors bright,
The fearless artist claims their light.
With passion burning, hearts set free,
Creating worlds for all to see.

The pulse of dreams within the frame,
Every canvas, a new name.
Brushes whisper, secrets shared,
Through realms of doubt, they're never scared.

Crafting visions, raw and true,
In hues of life, the artist grew.
With every splash, a story spun,
Through shades of grey and golden sun.

Emotions dance, both sharp and sweet,
In every heartbeat, art and heartbeat meet.
A chorus sings, through every hue,
The pulse of passion, fresh and new.

Together, we paint our souls awake,
In creations grand, the world we make.
With fearless hearts, we rise and claim,
The pulse of art, a timeless flame.

The Rhythm of Daring Journeys

In twilight's glow, we trace our way,
Through winding paths where shadows play.
With hearts alight, we dare to roam,
Each step we take, we claim our home.

The stars above, our guiding light,
In every challenge, we find our might.
Together forged, our spirits blend,
A journey's start, yet never end.

Through storms that howl and winds that bite,
We find our strength, we face the night.
The rhythm calls, a song so clear,
Adventure whispers, always near.

With every breath, a tale unfolds,
Of dreams we chase and truths we hold.
In moments raw, we seek what's real,
A tapestry of all we feel.

So let us dance, and let us sing,
In every heart, new hope will spring.
For daring journeys lead us true,
To skies renewed, to dreams anew.

Challenge the Quiet

In silence deep, a whisper calls,
To break the stillness, to rise, not fall.
With courage found in gentle sighs,
We light the world with open eyes.

The shadows loom, but do not fear,
For in the quiet, strength draws near.
Each heartbeat thumps, a steady drum,
A call to arms, to break the hum.

With words like fire, we spark the night,
Challenge the shadows, bring forth the light.
In every pause, a chance to learn,
For silence holds the will to burn.

With voices bold and spirits bright,
We rise as one, reclaim our might.
In every heart, a song awaits,
To challenge quiet, to open gates.

So let us stand, and let us shout,
Embrace the storm, erase the doubt.
With every voice that joins the song,
We challenge quiet, where we belong.

Fountains of Untold Stories

In valleys deep, where whispers flow,
Fountains rise, their tales bestow.
With every drop, a life unfolds,
A treasure trove of dreams retold.

Through hidden paths, the echoes ring,
Of ancient hearts and the songs they sing.
From every source, a spark ignites,
We gather close, embracing sights.

In shadows cast by twilight's hue,
The stories meld, create the new.
Each drop, a heartbeat intertwined,
In every soul, a tale unconfined.

With open hearts, we dive within,
From fountains deep, our journeys begin.
In every voice, a history thrives,
A melting pot of vibrant lives.

So let us drink from waters vast,
And weave the future from the past.
With every story shared, we grow,
In fountains pure, our spirits flow.

The Alchemy of Possibility

In quiet dreams, we paint the night,
With brush and heart, we craft our flight.
Transforming fears into pure gold,
An alchemist, both brave and bold.

Beneath the stars, our wishes gleam,
In every heartbeat, lives a dream.
With open hands, we mold our fate,
In every choice, we navigate.

Through trials hard, our spirits soar,
Possibilities we can't ignore.
With every step, a path we trace,
In every challenge, find our grace.

Like rivers flow, we shift and bend,
In alchemy, there's no true end.
With every loss, a chance to grow,
In every lesson, seeds we sow.

So let us dream and let us dare,
To shape the world, to freely share.
For in this dance of life, we see,
The alchemy of possibility.

Pathways of the Inventive

In shadows where ideas hide,
The spark of thought begins to glide.
With every twist, a new design,
A journey mapped in the divine.

Through tangled vines of dreams we weave,
The fabric of what we believe.
Innovation's call, a siren's song,
Invention's path, where we belong.

With paints of purpose, we will blend,
Unlock the doors that seem to end.
A world anew, from chaos born,
As pathways rise with each new dawn.

Digitized visions, bright and bold,
Stories of futures yet untold.
A light that flickers, then ignites,
The heart ignited, it takes flight.

Together we chase the fleeting light,
Each idea shining, pure and bright.
Through winding roads, we find our way,
In pathways of the inventive play.

Unmasking the Soul's Palette

Colors dance on life's rough stage,
Each stroke reveals a hidden page.
In shadows deep, our truths reside,
The palette broad, where feelings glide.

Through art we speak, in silent tones,
Unveiling depths, the heart's true stones.
Every hue, a story shared,
With each creation, we've declared.

As canvases of life unfold,
Emotions raw, and tales retold.
The brush, a wand, reveals our core,
In vivid shades, we seek for more.

With gentle hands, we shape and mold,
A journey through the brave and bold.
Reflecting dreams as colors blend,
In soul's palette, hearts transcend.

Impressions left, like whispers soft,
The beauty born from pain aloft.
Unmasking self is art's pure goal,
In every stroke, we find our soul.

Revolt of the Visual

Images clash and boldly fight,
Challenging norms with all their might.
Pixels collide in vibrant rage,
In revolt, they turn the page.

Abstract screams, and forms collide,
A vision quest, where rules subside.
Each color choice, a battle cry,
In this revolt, we learn to fly.

The lens distorts, reshapes the truth,
A fractured view that sparks the youth.
With every glance, the spectrum shifts,
Visual war, where art uplifts.

Through chaos blooms the pure divine,
A tapestry where all align.
The eyes, the windows, gazing wide,
In revolt of the visual tide.

Expressions rise, breaking the mold,
Revolutionary tales unfold.
With brush and lens, we shall ignite,
The power of a visual fight.

Storms of Inspiration

Winds of thought in tempest swirled,
Ideas clash, a brave new world.
Lightning strikes with vibrant thought,
In storms of muse, we seek what's sought.

A thunderous roar ignites the sky,
Catalyst for dreams held high.
With raindrops fall, the world we cleanse,
As storms of inspiration commence.

In swirling clouds, the vision forms,
Creativity breaks through the norms.
A flash of insight, fierce and true,
The calm that follows births anew.

With torrents fierce, the mind expands,
The chaos cradled in our hands.
As tempests dance, we find our note,
On waves of thoughts, we learn to float.

Embrace the storm, don't run or hide,
In winds of change, we take our stride.
Through storms of inspiration, we shall roam,
Each tempest guides us back to home.

Constellations of the Brave

In the night, stars whisper dare,
Brave souls rise, hearts laid bare.
With dreams like fires, they ignite the sky,
Breaking the darkness, letting hope fly.

Each heartbeat echoes tales untold,
Of warriors bold, hearts made of gold.
They chart their paths through cosmic streams,
Capturing legends, woven in dreams.

Through storms they journey, fearless and free,
Uniting as one, like the vast sea.
Every challenge faced with a fiery grin,
In the constellations, true stars begin.

Guided by light that never wanes,
They bear the burdens, share the pains.
Together they shimmer, through night and day,
Constellations of the brave lead the way.

They sail through tempests, rise from the grind,
In every struggle, new strength they find.
As they chart the skies with glimmers bright,
The brave shall always be the light.

The Awakening of the Unorthodox

In shadows deep, the bold arise,
With visions clear, and unyielding eyes.
Challenging norms with daring grace,
They dance to rhythms, the world must face.

Whispers echo in empty halls,
Unorthodox dreams break down the walls.
They paint with colors, vibrant and wild,
In every heart, they stir the child.

Thoughts unbound, they question the mold,
Against the current, they are bold.
In a world of silence, they choose to speak,
Their voices strong, their vision unique.

A symphony of change begins to play,
As the unorthodox forge their way.
Through laughter and tears, they amplify,
The beauty in truth, as they reach for the sky.

With every step, they redefine,
New paths emerge, in their design.
In the awakening, the brave take flight,
Unorthodox dreams, shining bright.

Art in Defiance of Fear

Brush meets canvas, a silent roar,
Colors clash, and spirits soar.
In strokes of courage, stories unfold,
Defying shadows, boldness takes hold.

With every line, a heart laid bare,
Art becomes armor against despair.
In whispered hues, they cast aside strife,
In every creation, they breathe life.

Sculpted dreams rise from stone cold night,
Chiseling fears, revealing light.
A dancer twirls, in grace she finds,
The rhythm of hope that unbinds minds.

With notes that echo through empty halls,
Music rises, breaking the walls.
An act of defiance, raw and clear,
Art becomes the voice, shedding fear.

In every piece, a world anew,
Expressions bold, bursting through.
Art in defiance, fierce and free,
A testament of strength, just let it be.

Builders of New Realities

With hands of purpose, they lay the ground,
Crafting visions where dreams are found.
Brick by brick, they shape the skies,
Builders of worlds, where hope never dies.

In the silence, ideas bloom,
Transforming spaces, dispelling gloom.
They sketch the future with fearless strokes,
Creating paths with ancient oaks.

Voices rise like towers high,
Through storms and trials, they soar and fly.
No limits bind them, nor chains confine,
Each dream a thread, in a grand design.

United in passion, they harness the light,
Illuminating shadows, igniting the night.
With every heartbeat, they craft a way,
Building new realms, come what may.

In the tapestry of time, they weave,
The fabric of futures, they dare believe.
Builders of new realities, strong and free,
In every heartbeat, a legacy.

Bold Strokes on Blank Canvases

In silence, the artist begins,
With colors that whisper of dreams.
Each stroke a statement, a roar,
A journey unfolds in bold seams.

Blank canvases wait for their fate,
With courage, the brush finds its way.
A riot of hues and passions collide,
Transforming the void in vivid display.

Brush dipped in hope, hearts unleashed,
As boundaries dissolve with each sweep.
Imagination dances on edges,
In wild abandon, deep shadows creep.

Layers of stories emerge from the mist,
Each stroke a piece of the soul's core.
With fervor, creation bursts forth,
In art, we find what we yearn for.

A masterpiece born from the fight,
In colors, the whispers find voice.
Each canvas, a tale of bold strokes,
And from silence, we boldly rejoice.

Fearless Imagination

In minds where wild visions roam,
Like birds in uncharted sky.
Free thoughts take flight without chains,
As wonders swirl and fly high.

With pens that dance on paper's skin,
Ideas spark like fireflies bright.
Fearless dreams cascade like rain,
Illuminating the veil of night.

In every twist and turn of fate,
Creativity finds a new door.
Bravely we share what's within,
A tapestry woven from lore.

Imagination, a fearless beast,
With whimsy and laughter entwined.
From depths of thoughts, magic unleashed,
In the garden of dreams, we're aligned.

With each new brushstroke of thought,
An echo of courage will rise.
Fearless, we pen our own tales,
Painting our truths without disguise.

Uncharted Paths of Expression

On roads less traveled, we roam,
With hearts that pulse like a drum.
Each step a whisper, a promise,
To realms where wild stories come.

Through valleys of shadows and light,
We carve our paths in the glow.
With each brush of emotion,
The seeds of our inner truth sow.

Voices rising, breaking the cage,
In echoes of courage we trust.
With every word, we embrace change,
And transform the silence to dust.

Mountains may tremble, seas may part,
As we venture into the new.
The maps of tomorrow are drawn
In colors that shimmer and hue.

On uncharted trails, we explore,
With visions that dance in the breeze.
In the art of expressing our souls,
We find our true selves, our release.

The Dance of Innovation

With sparks of genius in the air,
Innovation takes graceful leaps.
In rhythms of change, we engage,
As curiosity fuses and keeps.

Like dancers on a vibrant stage,
Ideas swirl in tempest wild.
From chaos, a pattern emerges,
Renewed by the hands of the child.

In every turn, a chance to grow,
A ballet of thoughts intertwined.
With courage, embrace the unknown,
For greatness is what we will find.

Melodies of progress resound,
As we paint outside of the lines.
In this dance, we break our chains,
Creating where passion entwines.

The future is written in steps,
Of daring, of dreams, and of play.
In the dance of innovation,
We rise, and together we sway.

The Alchemy of the Brave

In shadows deep, they find their might,
Forging dreams in the heart of night.
With every challenge, they rise anew,
Transforming fear into courage too.

Gold from grit, they sculpt their path,
Turning struggle into joyous wrath.
Each scar a story, a badge of war,
They walk on fire, seeking more.

In tempest's roar, they stand their ground,
With whispered chants, their spirits sound.
The fire within, a guiding star,
In the alchemy, they shine from afar.

Boundless hearts, unchained and free,
In the darkest hours, they find the key.
For in their veins, adventure flows,
The brave become legends, as courage grows.

Through trials faced, their essence gleams,
What once was lost, now builds their dreams.
Each step a note in their mighty song,
The alchemy of the brave will always belong.

Seasons of the Undaunted

In spring's embrace, hope takes its flight,
Undaunted souls chase the morning light.
With every bloom, they lift their gaze,
Renewing strength through summer's blaze.

As autumn leaves begin to fall,
They gather courage, heed the call.
In winter's chill, they find their fire,
The seasons blend in a dance of desire.

Unyielding grace in changing skies,
With every storm, their spirit flies.
The frost may bite, the storms may roar,
Yet undaunted hearts seek to explore.

Through trials faced, they craft their fate,
Turning doubt into something great.
For in each season, bonds they weave,
The undaunted rise, and they believe.

Together they stand, hand in hand,
Bound by dreams, they take a stand.
In every season, they find their way,
The undaunted shine through night and day.

Spark of the Unfettered

In the wild woods, where whispers dwell,
An unfettered spirit hears the bell.
With every heartbeat, a fire ignites,
A spark of freedom in endless nights.

They dance through shadows, fearless and bright,
Chasing horizons with pure delight.
Through tangled vines, they carve their course,
Fueled by passion, an inner force.

With every leap, they shatter chains,
The scent of freedom, in their veins.
In fields of dreams, they laugh and play,
The world's a canvas, they'll paint their way.

Their laughter rings like a bell of hope,
In the depths of despair, they learn to cope.
For within their souls, a fire burns clear,
The spark of the unfettered, with nothing to fear.

Together they rise, on wings of the bold,
In the heart of the night, their story unfolds.
With every light, they reach for the sky,
The spark of the unfettered, forever to fly.

A Symphony of the Audacious

In the dawn's hush, a symphony plays,
Audacious hearts in a rhythmic blaze.
With every note, they cast away doubt,
Crafting a melody, bold and sprout.

Through valleys deep, their voices soar,
Gathering strength, they yearn for more.
In the echoes of dreams, they find their sound,
A dance of the brave, where hopes are unbound.

With passion's fire, they challenge the night,
Striking chords that shimmer bright.
In the chorus of life, they find their role,
The audacious spirits sing from the soul.

Through every journey, their laughter rings,
In the symphony's heart, adventure springs.
With harmony, they embrace the unknown,
The audacious' call, a melody grown.

Together they rise, in cadence alive,
With every heartbeat, they learn to thrive.
A symphony played, from the edge of the fray,
The audacious dance, come what may.

Paths of Unfamiliar Comfort

In shadows softly whispering,
We tread on paths unknown,
With every step a new beginning,
In places we have grown.

Beneath the stars, our fears dissolve,
Among the leaves, we breathe,
Embrace the calm, let darkness solve,
The doubts that often seethe.

A gentle breeze will guide us near,
To corners of the heart,
Where fragments of our dreams appear,
And tender hopes depart.

In unfamiliar lands, we find,
The comforts of the soul,
As wisdom weaves through hearts entwined,
And makes the broken whole.

With each step, we rise anew,
In paths that we create,
For comfort lies in all we do,
In love that conquers fate.

The Pulse of Inspired Defiance

In the face of shadows looming,
We dare to take a stand,
With every heartbeat wildly blooming,
We craft our own command.

The pulse of hope, a throbbing force,
Through every doubt we rise,
Determined on our destined course,
With fire in our eyes.

Against the tides that try to drown,
We find our strength within,
With courage set upon our crown,
We refuse to yield or thin.

In unity, our voices swell,
A symphony of dreams,
With every challenge, we compel,
As freedom brightly gleams.

With hearts ablaze, we make our mark,
Inspired by the fight,
In defiance, we ignite the spark,
For justice, truth, and right.

Forge Your Own Story

With every choice, you craft your tale,
Each moment builds your fate,
Within the silence, hear the hail,
Of dreams that resonate.

Through valleys deep and mountains high,
Your journey paints the ground,
With ink of tears, and laughter's sigh,
Your legacy is found.

The pages turn, create your stride,
In chapters rich and bold,
Let passion be your trusted guide,
As life begins to unfold.

Embrace the storms, the calm, the light,
In all that you pursue,
For in the struggle, find your might,
And forge a world anew.

No one can write your story true,
But you alone can try,
With every pen stroke, find the view,
And let your spirit fly.

Lanterns in the Fog

In misty nights where dreams reside,
We wander through the grey,
With lanterns lit, our hearts our guide,
We chase the dawn's first ray.

The fog may hide the path ahead,
Yet faith will light the way,
With every flicker, hope is fed,
In shadows that delay.

Together, we navigate the haze,
With voices raised in song,
Through tangled woods and endless maze,
We'll find where we belong.

Each lantern shines a promise bright,
A spark against the gloom,
In unity, we spark the light,
And banish all the doom.

With courage found in tender hearts,
We'll brave the night's embrace,
For every journey slowly starts,
With love, we find our place.

A World in Technicolor

In shades of red and vibrant blue,
The skies above, they shift and hue.
Golden sunbeams warm the earth,
Each color sings of life and birth.

Fields of green stretch far and wide,
In every corner, dreams abide.
A palette rich, a canvas bright,
In this world, we find our light.

Whispers of lavender in the air,
Nature's art beyond compare.
Brushstrokes of clouds, a painted sea,
In every hue, we're bold and free.

Rivers of turquoise gently flow,
In this vision, our spirits grow.
From dusk till dawn, the colors play,
A world reborn with each new day.

In laughter shared, in love's embrace,
Technicolor fills each sacred space.
Together we weave this vibrant dream,
In harmony, we dance and gleam.

Sculpting with Heartfire

With hands that shape the molten clay,
We mold our hopes in bright array.
Each curve and edge a story told,
In every piece, our dreams unfold.

The kiln ignites with glowing light,
Transforming shadows into bright.
Sculpting passion, fierce and bold,
Heartfire burns, our spirits gold.

In silence deep, we carve our fate,
Chisels dance, emotions spate.
From stone and earth, we find our voice,
In artistry, we make our choice.

Layers rise, a texture vast,
Each finished work holds memories cast.
With every stroke, we breathe anew,
Heartfire's warmth ignites the true.

Together now, we shape our dreams,
In this raw art, the world redeems.
With passion fierce, our hearts ignite,
Sculpting life in love's pure light.

Hues of the Fearless Dreamer

In twilight's glow, the dreamers rise,
With palettes bright beneath the skies.
With fearless strokes, they paint their fate,
In every shade, they celebrate.

Emerald greens and shades of gold,
Stories of courage bravely told.
A canvas rich, a bold frontier,
In every hue, they cast out fear.

The past behind, the future vast,
In swirls of colors, shadows cast.
Fearless hearts unleash their might,
In every brushstroke, pure delight.

From dusky hues to vibrant dawn,
A journey rich, where dreams are drawn.
With colors fresh, they seize the day,
Hues of passion lead the way.

Together we dance on this bright page,
Fearless dreamers, we break the cage.
In every dream, we leave our mark,
With hues of joy, we light the dark.

Dance of the Fearless Mind

In rhythms deep, the heartbeats sway,
A fearless mind leads the way.
With thoughts like stars in night's embrace,
We dance through shadows, find our place.

The mind's ballet, a playful flight,
Through ideas bold we chase the light.
In spirals bright, we spin and leap,
Awakening dreams from slumber deep.

With every step, we break the chains,
In daring leaps, release our pains.
A choreography of the brave,
In this dance, the soul can save.

Creation flows in every beat,
The fearless mind won't know defeat.
With courage found, we redefine,
In each bold move, the world aligns.

Together, we soar through realms untold,
In the dance of wisdom, fierce and bold.
With every thought a spark ignites,
Lighting the path on starry nights.

9 789916 877456